learned
LEADERSHIP

Leaders are not **born**, they're **made**.
Discover **10 keys** to
awakening the leader within you.

Greg Kozera

Copyright © 2007 by Greg Kozera

All rights reserved. No part of this book may be used or reproduced in any manner whatsoever without prior written consent of the author, except as provided by the United States of America copyright law.

Published by Advantage, Charleston, South Carolina.
Member of Advantage Media Group.

ADVANTAGE is a registered trademark and the Advantage colophon is a trademark of Advantage Media Group, Inc.

Printed in the United States of America

ISBN: 978-1-59932-021-2

> Most Advantage Media Group titles are available at special quantity discounts for bulk purchases for sales promotions, premiums, fundraising, and educational use. Special versions or book excerpts can also be created to fit specific needs.
>
> For more information, please write: Special Markets, Advantage Media Group, P.O. Box 272, Charleston, SC 29402 or call 1.866.775.1696.

learned
LEADERSHIP

To my parents who gave me the values that I have written about, my wife and children for their support and encouragement, Bruce for showing me leadership by example and allowing me to try my ideas and finally to my friends at the National Speakers Association and the Ohio Chapter especially Barb, David, Jon, Ken, and Toni who encouraged me and allowed me to be accountable to them. Without all of you this book would still be just a wish.

TABLE OF CONTENTS

INTRODUCTION   **WHAT IS LEADERSHIP?** | 9

CHAPTER 1   **VISION** | 15
If you know where you are going people will follow

CHAPTER 2   **PASSION** | 21
If you get excited so will others

CHAPTER 3   **ATTITUDE** | 25
Your people will reflect yours

CHAPTER 4   **ACTION** | 29
This implements your vision

CHAPTER 5   **TRUST** | 33
You can't lead without it

CHAPTER 6   **TEAMBUILDING** | 39
You can't do it alone

CHAPTER 7   **COURAGE** | 45
Leadership is not for wimps

CHAPTER 8   **INFLUENCE** | 49
What you do speaks louder than what you say

CHAPTER 9   **RESPONSIBILITY** | 61
Taking this will actually give you control

CHAPTER 10   **DEVELOPING PEOPLE AND FUTURE LEADERS** | 65
Investing time in people pays big dividends. Pass on what you know

CLOSING THOUGHTS | 69

WHAT NOW? | 73

INTRODUCTION

It was November 1999 on a cool crisp evening in Wheeling, West Virginia. The grass was lush and manicured. The lines freshly painted. The stands were packed. It was the semifinals of the West Virginia Boy's State Soccer Tournament and we were there for the first time in the history of our small high school. As our boys were doing their warm up laps, I walked around the field and just savored the moment. I remember thinking, "I wish my kids had been able to experience this." All three of my kids had played high school soccer for our school. I was a supportive team parent during those years. My youngest son's team had the only undefeated regular season in school history but lost in the sectionals. Bruce, the head coach, and I, his assistant, started coaching the next season.

In West Virginia high school soccer there are no classes by school size so to get to the state Final Four you must beat the biggest and the best schools in the state. This wasn't supposed to be our year. The previous year we had a talented team loaded with seniors and never got out of our section.

In 1998 we had what we thought was a great team loaded with experienced seniors and talent. We had a good year but not the great year we expected. What was so special about this year's team with only four seniors and a lot of inexperience?

What was missing from the other teams? Bruce and I talked about that. As a small school I actually thought that maybe we couldn't compete with the big schools because they had a larger talent pool of players. But was there another reason we never made it to the state final four? In high school sports we have always heard about "Senior Leadership" and how important it is to a team's success. Did our seniors really understand leadership? If they didn't was this the missing link to our success? We assumed that they knew how to lead. But where do seniors learn leadership from? Even in business where do most people learn leadership from? If they learn anything at all, typically it is from watching those that preceded them. More often than not they will follow what others have done in the area of leadership, like the previous year's seniors, maybe their coaches or in business their pervious manager(s). This could be good or bad depending on what type of leader they are imitating. Bruce and I thought, "What would happen if we taught our seniors leadership?"

In 1999 we made a decision to work with our high school seniors on leadership. We began a process called "Senior Minutes." Immediately following each practice we gave a brief lesson on leadership to our seniors. The only problem was in 1999 we only had four seniors. Almost all of our starters and experience were gone. We were "rebuilding." After some leadership lessons I asked these four seniors, "What is your goal for this season." They responded, "Coach, we want to play for the state title." I was stunned. In the history of our school in soccer (over fifteen years) we had never been to the state tournament. We made it out of our section to the regional tournament only once and got beat there. A few years previous we had achieved a remarkable undefeated regular season but lost to our arch rival, a large AAA school, in the section final. I was thinking that just having a winning season would be great and these four guys were going for the state title. I'm not going to tell anyone they can't achieve their dream so my response was simply, "Ok. We've got some work to do."

That season proved to be magical. After playing an unforgettable semifinal game where we beat the second ranked team in the state (they started ten seniors) in the end *we did it. We played for the state championship!!*

Looking back on that first season we ever went to the state final four one thing was clear—our seniors really were leaders on the field and in practice. Those four young men, in particular the captain, BJ, had developed into strong leaders and because of that they overcame incredible obstacles to accomplish the improbable.

We have continued these "senior minutes" and have seen many of our seniors develop into strong leaders. We discovered that leadership is not a skill that we are born with but a skill that can be learned. The world today needs good leaders. In the business world I see many good managers but very few leaders. We manage things but we lead people. Business today needs both good management and strong leadership. Things are far more predictable than people and this makes leadership far more difficult than management. Many organizations confuse the two terms. People finish a management school or seminar and are referred to as leaders. This may or may not be true. They may be in a leadership position but are they really leaders? Are they influencing people or commanding them? Can they develop people? One test I use for a leader is if a person didn't have a title, or wasn't the boss with the power to fire or give raises would people still follow them? If they would then I consider them a leader.

Think of the people that lead successful volunteer organizations or groups or even successful network marketing organizations. They can fire people (I guess) but then they wouldn't have an organization. They can't give raises. They can't command or demand because their people can leave at any time because they are involved by choice. They have to be leaders in order to be successful because the only real power they have is the power to lead and have others follow by choice.

How important is leadership to your success? It depends on what you want. A friend of mine in the energy industry, John, is a very successful engineer, and he told me a story about his brother. John's brother is also a graduate engineer two years older than him. John said that his brother's grades were only average in college, well below John's. John's brother now is an executive with a multinational oil company. He makes big bucks and owns several homes including a ranch in the western United States.

I asked, "How did that happen?" John said that both he an his brother played baseball in college and, "While the rest of us guys were in the locker room flipping towels at each other my brother was always in talking to the coach." In short his brother was learning about leadership and now he is a rich executive and his "smarter" brother is still an engineer. Companies are looking for leaders and will pay for them.

The purpose of this book is to help new leaders whether they are in business, athletics, volunteer organizations, school or just trying to learn how to lead and understand what leadership is. It will help them to believe that they can learn to lead effectively if they choose to, and will give them some methods and ideas they can use to develop their own leadership skills.

Remember leadership is a learnable skill. Our seniors in 1999 were sharp kids and hard workers. Once they developed their leadership skills they were able to achieve their dreams and others followed them to achieve their own dreams. You can learn how to lead effectively if you choose to.

WHAT IS LEADERSHIP?

Recently I was at the annual convention of the National Speakers Association. The place was full of famous entertainers, speakers and authors. I felt like a midget among giants. During the convention I had an opportunity to meet informally with a number of professionals who spoke on leadership or did leadership training. Their answer to the question "What is a leader?" was fairly simple. "Anyone who influences and develops people is a leader." Notice there isn't any mention of title like president, chief executive officer (CEO) or team captain. Everyone agreed that leadership isn't a title. Leadership can come from *anywhere* in an organization. The person that can influence the CEO and develop him or her the way they choose is the real leader even though they don't have the title.

A good friend of mine played on a high school football team that won the state championship. He told me that the seniors got together and decided the state championship was their goal for that season. They then convinced the rest of the team and the coaching staff that as a team they could do it. The seniors were the leaders and they developed the rest of the team.

When I asked him, "Did you like everyone on the team?" He said, "Heck no. Some of the guys were jerks. But when we were on the field we were going for the same goal and it didn't matter. We played as a team."

Mother Theresa of Calcutta had no title and no real power but was a great leader. She influenced thousands to support her ministry to the poor and dying in India. She developed a group of leaders to carry on her ministry after her death. Mother Theresa also influenced millions of people on the planet to look at their own values and change how they look at human life and consider treating all life with dignity and respect. It's not about title or position.

Are some people born leaders? It is true that some people are born with skills that may help them to be leaders. Other may be born into family or position where it may be expected like the Kennedy's or the Royal Family in some countries. The reality is that leaders are developed. Leadership is a skill like any other that can be *learned* if we choose. Our attitude, our ability to believe in the future to have a positive vision is critical to being a good leader. The ability to believe in people is also important. Leaders know that they can't do everything themselves. They need people to accomplish and carry out their vision. So the ability to work with people and build teams is also important. These are also skills that can be learned.

So why would someone follow you? If someone gave you a title of "manager" or "team captain" people may follow you for a while but they won't follow you through the tough times if all you have is a title. If people like you they will follow you. This might be like the class president. The election of class officers is a popularity contest most of the time. We give the officers permission to lead us because we like them. If we are not careful we can allow our national or local elections to become popularity contests rather than looking at candidates' ideas, philosophy or qualifications.

A higher level of leadership is following people because of what they have done for us as individuals. People will also follow you because of what you have done for the organization. This might be the Team Captain that is also a strong player that has led the team to past victories or people follow the manager that gets promoted to VP because of their success as a manager. People will follow you because they like your vision and want to be part of it. They must believe that you can do what you say you will do. They may also follow you because they believe that they will achieve their dreams and personal success by following you.

There are many leadership styles. Mother Theresa's style was different than Donald Trump's or President Ronald Reagan's or Bill Cowher who led the Pittsburgh Steelers to a Super Bowl Championship. We may think that we have to be tough and competitive to be an effective leader. Maybe even scream a little. Not so. My daughter lead our high school youth group, held other leadership positions in high school and college including captain of her college soccer team. Since she graduated and has been working she was named a team leader of her teaching team at school over people with more time and experience. The teams and groups she has lead are usually very successful. We were talking one day and she surprised me when she said, "I hate to see anyone lose. In college I wish every game could have ended in a tie." Of course in college every game didn't end in a tie. Her team played hard and won their share of games. But considering her background of competitive sports it wasn't a statement I expected. Actually her philosophy may be the reason that she is an effective leader. She is always looking for win/win solutions instead of win/lose.

There are many leadership styles; not just one. Your style will be a function of your personality and the skills you have. You don't need to be like anyone but you. However, even though there are many styles there are certain things that are true of all leaders. That is what this book is all about. Remember leadership is a learned skill. You can be a leader if you choose. Leadership isn't about power or position. If you can influence people and develop people you are a leader. If you want to be a leader read on. The ideas presented in this book if practiced will help you to develop you own leadership skills. Your personality will then give you your own unique leadership style.

Some ideas on how to best use this book

As leaders it is our actions that make the difference in our lives and the lives of those we lead. At the end of each chapter are some, ***Thoughts to ponder and actions to take*** . It is important to not just to read these but to take the actions. You may find it easier to read this book through in its entirety and then work on the actions by rereading a chapter a day and taking the actions. This book is also designed to be used as a reference and teaching tool. We suggest not just reading it once but keep it where you can refer to it as you develop your leadership skills and are faced with challenges. You can also share the information with others especially people that you are training to be leaders in your organization or team. If you are training your leaders you can use it as a training aid. We typically cover a chapter a day although some topics require several days. Encourage those you are training to take the actions at the end of each chapter. These can be used as assignments and the results can be discussed individually or in a group setting. Monitor the progress that you or you group is making. Encourage and praise them for their successes. It is always gratifying for me to watch as our seniors become effective leaders in a relatively short period of time.

CHAPTER 1

VISION

IF YOU KNOW WHERE YOU ARE GOING PEOPLE WILL FOLLOW.

Vision isn't seeing with our eyes it is seeing with our mind and heart. The great leader sees into the future. He or she sees where they want to be. Sometimes we call it a dream. Walt Disney saw Disneyland and Disney World long before they were constructed. He described EPCOT in great detail and when it opened in 1982 it was very close to his vision. Walt died sixteen years before that in 1966 but the vision lived on. Dr. Martin Luther King Jr. said, "I have a dream." President John F. Kennedy "saw" Americans on the moon by the end of the 1960s. Even though he didn't live to see it his vision inspired a nation and against the odds they made it happen. That's how powerful a leader's vision can be.

I remember as a junior high school student in the 1960s our science teacher was talking about all the challenges and how hard it would be to put men on the moon and get them home safely. I remember thinking, "So what, we're Americans we'll figure out how to do it." People at NASA happily worked overtime without pay because they were so caught up in the vision President Kennedy had cast. I remember sitting around our TV with my entire family on the evening of July 20, 1969 as with excitement we watched Neil Armstrong become the first person to set foot on the moon.

People will follow us or not follow us because of our vision. This can be as simple as what to do on Friday night, where we want our team to be at the end of the season or what we want our company to accomplish this year. One of my favorite questions for a CEO is, "If we are sitting here talking at this time next year and this was a great year, what will have happened?" If people are excited by our vision and know that we are committed to achieving it they will follow. As leaders we must always see things first in our mind so that we can help our people to create them with action.

How is vision different from a goal? I think of vision as the big picture, the ultimate destination. Goals are the steps along the way that we need to reach to achieve it. A goal might be filling certain positions with competent people so that we will have a solid team or having a certain level of conditioning or a certain monthly revenue goal. These are achievable goals on the way to the vision.

When our high school soccer team got together to start practice in the fall of 2004 we had a lot of new faces. We lost our twelve seniors from the previous season and in addition we had lost two all-state players who had transferred. We were left with one returning starter. We only had four seniors and three juniors. The majority of our roster was made up of freshmen and sophomores, few of whom had ever even played in a varsity game. We were faced with our usual challenging schedule.

After several weeks of practice I asked the seniors at our leadership moment after practice, "Where do you want to be at the end of the season." Their answer was quick and certain. "We want to go to the State Final Four." Was this realistic? No of course not. A .500 season was realistic. But I wasn't about to tell them that. So my response was simply. "We have some work to do." They really believed it could happen. After losing our first two games we went on to a 12-7-2 record. We were ranked 12th in the final state rankings. Five players won All State or All Region honors. Unfortunately we lost in the playoffs to the defending state champs who were also the number 1 ranked team in the state.

So what happened? Why would a team that should logically only be a .500 team do so well? There were several reasons but the biggest reason is they never thought of themselves as an average team. They thought of themselves as contenders. They aimed high. They may have missed their goal but they finished much better than anyone (excluding themselves) expected.

It was the vision of our seniors and the captain, BJ in particular, that drove our 1999 team to play for the state title. After every practice I asked, "What's our vision?" They would scream, "To play for the state title." Eventually they all began to believe it. When we were down 0-2 at the half of the state semifinal game my question at half time was. "What's our vision?" Their answer was, "To play for the state title." Then I asked, "What's our goal." They responded, "To beat St. Joe." It fired up their belief in themselves, and we did play for the state title.

Our soccer players always know what the vision is. They are reminded daily. It is amazing how many organizations and companies either don't have a vision or the "leadership" hasn't communicated it to the rest of the organization. Leaders have a vision and communicate it. Managers don't.

As a leader your team must know the vision. Vision is a road map that helps you and your team or organization know the final destination. Just like a road map there are multiple routes to any destination, there are different ways to achieve the vision. As long as everyone knows the destination they can help you to get there.

Dr. Benjamin Mays, the mentor for Dr. Martin Luther King Jr., said that it is okay not to reach your goal, as long as you have a goal to reach for. What is sinful is low aim that is setting our goals too low. When we aim too low we can never reach the potential we were created for. When we aim high we bring our subconscious mind into play that doesn't know the difference between what is real and what isn't.

So what is a realistic vision? Is it thirteen colonies that decided to declare independence from England, the most powerful nation on earth in 1776? What about John F. Kennedy who declared in 1961 we will put a man on the moon by the end of the decade and bring him safely home? At the time he had no clue how because we didn't have the capability. We couldn't even launch a rocket without blowing it up. What about the girl who lost her arm to a shark that still wins the national surfing championship? All of the above happened and all would have been considered unrealistic by some people. Our trip to the state final four in 1999 would have been considered unrealistic by most people. Even my first thoughts were, "That's not realistic". But our 4 seniors believed in their vision. That belief was contagious especially when we began to have success. Eventually they had the team convinced we could do it. That is the power of leadership and a vision. Personally I believe that God wouldn't give us a vision (not just a wish) without the potential to achieve it. At Walt Disney World I always hear, "If you can dream it you can do it." That means that nothing is impossible. I think that the impossible just takes a little longer and a little more effort.

What does this all mean for potential leaders? I suggest that you never be afraid to dream and aim high. Sometimes the only way to know what we are truly capable of is to test our limits by going after our highest dreams.

Having a vision as a leader is critical but just as critical is that we must truly believe in our heart and subconscious mind that it will happen. In 2005 we were ranked in the top 10 in our state and were getting ready to play the number one ranked team in the state. They were undefeated and would score over 100 goals that season as a team. Unfortunately we had just lost our leading goal scorer to a knee injury. One of our other 2 seniors had ripped his leg open on a rock on the field in the previous game. To make matters worse we were going to play them on Saturday and Friday night we watched them demolish another top 10 team. I was worried that our team might lose confidence. As our team was leaving the stadium after watching the game I pulled the junior aside that we had just promoted to captain because of the injuries. "What do you think?" I asked. He looked me in the eyes and said, "We can take them coach." He was serious. He also scored the only goal the next day in a great display of heart, teamwork and leadership that included our injured players. We handed the number one team in the state its only loss and shutout of the regular season. It started with the belief of our leaders.

Henry Ford said, "If you think you can or think you can't you're right." As unrealistic as some of the above may have sounded at the time I would guess that in every case success was no surprise to the leaders because they believed in their vision and expected success. How often have you ever won or succeeded when you expected to lose or fail? I can't think of any in my life. If we don't believe in our own vision, can we expect others to believe in it? What can we do to develop the belief we need to achieve our vision? These thoughts may help you;

- Start with small successes. If you want to run five miles for the first time you need to run one mile successfully. That may give you the belief to run two miles and so forth.

- Hang out with positive people who will support and encourage you. This book would not have been written without the encouragement of my friends at the Ohio Chapter of the National Speakers Association. They believed in me and told me why I could be successful. We all have self doubts. We need people who believe in us to help us to keep believing in ourselves.

- Read positive books and listen to positive tapes or CDs. Leaders are readers. I have been in the offices of CEOs and other executives and always find books. Listening to executives I find that they all read. What we put into our mind not only gives us knowledge but can help us keep our attitude positive helping us to believe in our ability to achieve our vision.

- Do something positive on a daily basis toward your vision. They key is daily. This gives you the opportunity for those successes. Each success builds your belief and moves you closer to your vision.

As leaders how do we know what we really can attain? How do we know if we are really reaching our potential and that of our team or just going for what is easily attainable? Sometimes we may need to stretch, aim higher than usual even if we fail. That can be scary but what is worse than failure is aiming low and succeeding because we never grow to our potential. Even if we fail at first it is important to try again. If we look at the lives of successful individuals and even teams we find that practically all failed before they achieved their great success or break through. We might also look at what we are passionate about. What gets us excited or motivated? We need to be excited and motivated first if we expect those that follow us to be. Is there something we always wanted to do or achieve? Remember what Dr. Mays said that even if we do fail to reach our vision if we have aimed high enough we will find ourselves much better off than if we had aimed low and achieved what is safe or average. The greatest successes we will have as leaders are when we aim high like the great leaders do.

What great things would happen in our lives and those who follow us if we really stretched and aimed for some goals that were maybe a little "unrealistic"? My players didn't think they were being unrealistic when they decided to shoot for the final four. Some might call them overachievers. They just aimed high, believed, worked hard, played as a team and found their real potential. As leaders we all can too if we're not afraid to aim a little higher and we can take others with us.

One of the most powerful exercises we can do as leaders is to write our vision and goals down and read them periodically. This keeps them fresh in our thoughts and allows our powerful subconscious mind to work on them. This also helps us to stay focused on them. The first time we did this as a family was powerful. We sat around the kitchen table and decided what we wanted to accomplish in the next year. We wrote everything down. I stuck the paper in my briefcase. That year we didn't even read it but when I pulled the paper out a year later I was shocked at how many of the goals we had accomplished. Write it down!

As leaders we must have a dream or vision. This gives us direction and if others know that we believe in our dream or vision they will follow us. Have a dream and make it a big dream.

THOUGHTS *to ponder and* ACTIONS *to take*

- Do I have a dream or vision for my team or organization?

- Do I believe that we can achieve it?

- Have I written it down? Do I read it daily?

- Does my team or organization know what my vision is?

- How high do I aim? Am I guilty of constantly having low aim?

- This week write down your dreams or vision and read them.

- Set a goal that is just outside your comfort zone.

- Talk to your team about your vision this week. Make sure they know what it is.

CHAPTER 2

PASSION

IF YOU GET EXCITED SO WILL OTHERS.

Rich was one of my friends growing up. He also tended to be the one we followed. If Rich suggested an activity like playing war, going to see a movie or playing a game we did it. The other guys in our group could suggest something to do and if Rich didn't agree it didn't happen. Rich was our leader. He always seemed to have great ideas. But maybe the big difference between Rich and the rest of us was his passion. When Rich was describing what he wanted to do you could see the excitement in his face and feel it in his voice. We could see ourselves having a lot of fun and when we followed Rich we usually did. Passion is a quality of all great leaders. Leaders need to have a vision but their passion for their vision is what excites people and makes others want to follow them.

President John F. Kennedy inspired us to go to the moon. Martin Luther King Jr. had a dream for brotherhood and equality for all people. Mother Theresa believed in the dignity of all human life and Ronald Reagan's passion for freedom led to the dismantling of the Berlin wall and the end of the Cold War. These are just a few leaders who were passionate about their vision and not only inspired people to follow them but inspired people to continue to follow their vision even after their deaths.

When our high school soccer team was playing in its first ever state semi-final game we were behind 0-2 after three quarters to the number two ranked team in the state. They were loaded with talent and most of their players were seniors. To make matters worse they had allowed only nine goals all season. We were a great team but we didn't have their experience or talent and now we only had twenty minutes to score at least twice against them. At the end of the third quarter our captain, BJ, was on the ground hurt and being worked on by the trainer. Bruce, our head coach, walked over to see how BJ was. The look on Bruce's face was of grave concern. BJ looked up at Bruce, pointed right at him and with fire in his eyes and teeth gritted he practically shouted, "Don't you *dare* take me out coach." I can picture that scene as if it were yesterday. The entire team saw what had happened. They were also tired and hurting. Whether he realized it or not BJ had sent a message to his players. By his actions he had told his team that even though he was hurting and we were behind he wasn't about to quit. This is leadership by example. BJ's passion was apparent. They could see it in his eyes and his determined walk. They heard it in his voice. I don't recall giving a motivational talk at the end of the 3rd quarter. I didn't need to. BJ's passion said it all. Our vision for that season was to play for the state title. BJ's passion told the team that he not only wasn't about to quit but he still believed that we could win. His players followed him back onto the field and in an incredible fourth quarter we came back to tie the game and finally win in overtime to achieve our vision and play for the state title. Passion is powerful.

I was recently at a trade association meeting where the president of the organization was trying to increase membership and complained to the group that their industry didn't have the passion that people from other organizations had. He recounted a story of a young lady who took a vacation and was paying her own expenses to fly to Washington, DC to lobby for her cause. Apparently his members weren't willing to do that. I could easily see the problem. It was him, the leader. If he had passion for his association and its causes, I couldn't tell. You couldn't hear any passion in his monotone voice or in his facial expressions. He may have been passionate about his industry and its cause but he needed to tell his face so that the rest of the organization could sense it and be moved to action. I found out that nothing changed as a result of his appeal.

Passion is emotional. You as the leader must first feel it. One can't expect any leader to be passionate about everything. But the leader must be passionate about their vision if they expect others to believe in it too and follow them. When the leader thinks about their vision it should excite them. BJ's passion to play for the state title didn't start in that semifinal game. It was there for most of the season including practice. One way to understand passion is to talk to anyone who is really excited or passionate about their dream or vision. All you have to do is ask a question and they will tell you all about it. Listen to the tone of their voice see if you can sense the passion. Look at their eyes and facial expressions. If you know someone that has just fallen in love you can get a sense for their passion when they start talking about their lover. You can feel it.

Passion cannot be taught. Your vision must excite you and no one can do that for you. But remember, just like a relationship, love and passion develop over time. In a relationship we have to put something into it if we want something out of it. In the same way passion for our vision deepens as we invest in it and start to "see" ourselves achieving it. I challenge you to let yourself get excited about something. Just let it happen without suppressing your emotions. Think about what excites you when you think about it. It might be your favorite sport like surfing, skiing, fishing, football or hunting. In West Virginia, I know hunters who talk about deer season all year long. Your passion might be the one you love (I hope there is a little passion here), your kids, some special project or cause you are involved with, or maybe your next vacation. If you can get passionate about something and show it when you are talking to others, you can probably get excited and passionate about your vision. If achieving your vision doesn't excite you maybe you need to rethink it, or maybe you don't believe your vision is achievable. A mentor may be helpful to you in this situation. I challenge you to find your passion.

Can you lead without passion? Yes you can. Some people just aren't passionate or maybe they are afraid to show their emotions. (We'll talk about courage later.) Some people are naturally unemotional. Just like that association president I told you about. Their trade association is well run and reasonably successful. I believe that the president is probably a leader. I also believe that if he was outwardly excited and passionate about his vision of association growth his membership would be inspired and excited. At that point the president may become a great leader. Passion helps people to believe in the vision. People like to be part of an organization that is going places. Successful teams don't have problems getting members. Everyone likes to be part of a winner. I believe passion is the difference between a good leader and a great leader. Jesus was a great leader. Jesus' organization continues to grow and is over 2000 years old. Its members number in the millions and he started with twelve followers.

One of my favorite Bible stories is "The walk to Emmaus" in Luke 24:13-35. It was after the resurrection and Jesus began walking with two of his followers who did not immediately recognize him. Once Jesus had disappeared from their sight they said, "Wasn't it like a fire burning in us when he talked to us on the road."

That's passion, and they were spurred to action by it. One sign of great leaders is when they can get others excited about their vision. Their followers will then act to help make it happen.

So as a leader have a vision, believe it can happen and get excited and passionate about it. Your people will follow you and if you can instill even a little of your passion for your vision in them they will act to help you to make it happen.

THOUGHTS *to ponder and* ACTIONS *to take*

- What are you passionate about or what excites you? Try to name five things.

- Think about how these five things make you feel.

- Does your vision get you excited?

- Do people sense your passion?

- Check yourself out today by standing in front of a mirror and think about your vision. Talk about your vision (silent self talk is okay if you are worried about what others might think). Can you see passion in your face and your eyes?

- Tape yourself talking about your vision. Can you hear any passion in your voice?

- Would you follow you?

CHAPTER 3

ATTITUDE

YOUR PEOPLE WILL REFLECT YOURS.

Everyone has the capability to make people happy. Some people do it by entering a room. Others do it by leaving a room. I know both types of people and I'll bet you do too. One place I worked there was a certain guy who would come up to your cubicle and just start talking. Most of his talk was pretty negative and boring. Everyone felt the same way about him. It got so bad that we all agreed if he was talking to one of your neighbors and you knew it, you were to call the person. Once the phone started to ring he would say goodbye and leave. I thought about that years later and it was kind of sad. The poor guy never figured it out. None of us at the time could figure out how to help him.

There are some people that we just like to be around. They are happy and they make us happy. They encourage us and make us feel better about ourselves. If they are leading us and there is a problem, we know that we will be okay.

One of the biggest differences in people is their attitude. Organizations typically reflect the attitudes of their management or leaders. I was at a popular ice cream store recently with my grandkids and the line had to be ten people deep, there was only one girl, about high school age, all by herself behind the counter. She had to get the ice cream and run the register. She had every reason to be cross because all of the people weren't nice to her and of course there were those that just couldn't make up their minds. This girl had a smile and friendly greeting for everyone. I watched her work while we ate our ice cream. The line stayed ten deep, but she was still working hard. She even started singing.

Remarkable, I thought.

Her attitude doesn't just leave a positive impression of her but it reflects positively on her company. Maybe it even reflects the attitude of her company.

Attitude is how we see the world. Is the glass half empty or is it half full? Are people basically good or are they not to be trusted? Are we positive or negative about our world? Are we happy most of the time or do other people or circumstances determine our happiness? Do we smile? Do we see problems as temporary distractions, opportunities or detours on the way to our dreams, or do we see them as roadblocks or catastrophes that are out to destroy us?

Recently at Walt Disney World, I was standing in line to buy some cold drinks on a typical hot sunny day. The young lady running the stand smiled and asked the man in front of me, "How are you?" Well he told her. All he could do was complain about the weather and how hot it was. When she asked me I smiled and said, "I'm excellent. I'm on vacation and I'm glad to be here." Our attitude is all about how we see the world. The weather was the same for both of us. We just saw things differently.

Our success as a leader will largely be determined by our attitude. Let's face it would you follow someone who you were happy to see them leave? Your attitude will determine whether people will choose to follow you. Remember BJ, our captain, the players didn't always like him because he made them work hard, but they followed him, in part, because of his attitude. They knew he wanted to win and so did they. They knew he really believed our dream. They knew he believed in them.

Here is the best part about attitude. We get to choose to be happy, positive and see people as basically good. One thing I notice is that the higher you go in any successful organization, the better the attitudes are. These people don't have great attitudes because of their success. They have success because of their great attitudes. People with great attitudes seem to rise to the top. As a leader, our people will tend to reflect our attitude. If we don't like the attitude of most of the people who work for us, we might want to check our own attitude.

So how can we develop a great attitude? Here are some ideas that you may find helpful.

- Hang out with people with great attitudes. We tend to become like those we spend time with. If we spend time with negative people or people with bad attitudes we will be just like them. We can choose to find and hang out with people with good attitudes that are positive. I always make a point to go to my National Speakers Association chapter meetings and annual conventions. Just being in a room with hundreds of people that are positive, encouraging and know they are going somewhere, can't help but have a positive effect on me. I always leave those meetings, uplifted, energized and with an improved attitude.

- Watch what goes into our brain. What are we reading or watching on TV? How much positive news or encouragement do we get from the morning news? After watching the morning news are you excited or depressed? We need to be informed but do we need to hear the same depressing stories for the third time? Read something positive every day. The best times to read are first thing in the morning to start our day and set our attitude and/or just before we go to bed to let our subconscious mind work on those positive thoughts all night long. There are lots of great books. Leaders are readers. We can also listen to positive audio tapes or CDs. We can help our attitude while we are driving or working.

- Make a point to smile more. This is also contagious. Try looking in a mirror and smiling for thirty seconds or more even if you don't feel like smiling. You will probably find yourself starting to feel happy. I don't know why it works but it does.

- Take care of yourself. Get enough sleep, exercise and eat a proper diet with enough vitamins and minerals. Taking care of yourself will give you energy and help your attitude.

- Make time for yourself. A vacation, a long weekend or just 15-20 minutes of quiet time a day will help you relax and recharge and will help your attitude.

Having a great attitude is critical for any leader. If people are going to follow you they need to like being around you. The better your attitude the more successful you will find yourself. Your attitude is not determined by what happens to you it is a daily choice. Having a great attitude will help you through adversity. It will help you to develop your ability to influence your people because they will reflect your attitude. You choose your attitude and you can change your attitude. Remember as a leader your attitude will influence the attitudes of those you lead. Make your attitude and theirs positive.

THOUGHTS *to ponder and* ACTIONS *to take*

- How do you make people happy most of the time? Is it when they see you coming or when they see you leaving?

- Do I take care of my body and my mind? If yes great! If not make a decision to start this week.

- How is my attitude? What might I need to change?

- Who do I spend most of my time with? How do they affect my attitude?

- This week make a point to be aware of what goes into my mind. (TV, movies newspapers, books, conversations) If you don't already read make a point to start. Remember leaders are readers. Find a positive motivational or inspirational book and make a point to start reading it. Every great journey starts with a single step.

CHAPTER 4

ACTION

THIS IMPLEMENTS YOUR VISION.

How can you tell when a leader is around? Simple, things happen. In 1999 whether it was practice or a game, BJ made things happen. Even in practice when BJ was leading a drill our players were working. They didn't always like it or appreciate it but they followed him. Think of the great leaders like President Franklin Roosevelt, who led our nation during World War II, Martin Luther King Jr., Mother Theresa, Susan B. Anthony (who helped women gain the right to vote), President Ronald Reagan and even the entrepreneur, Donald Trump they all changed the world by making things happen. Leaders are doers. They are people of action.

There is a time to talk, a time to think and plan and finally a time to act. I worked with one manager who was afraid of making a mistake. We were looking at doing an expansion and there were several options. We talked a lot. We gathered the facts and looked at the pros and cons of the options. We needed the expansion but my manager couldn't decide. He wouldn't act. Finally the regional manager showed up and decided for him. The regional manager took the lead to make things happen. We probably all know people that talk a good game. They have great ideas and plans but they never happen because these people never do the work it takes to make them happen. They don't take action.

At the end of the day it is all about what we *do* that will determine our level of success as leaders. We can know what to do, but unless we actually do something nothing happens.

Why don't potential leaders act? Here are some possible reasons.

- *Fear.* This is the number one reason for inaction. This could be fear of failure. Fear of making the wrong decision. Fear of what people might think or say. Fear of any number of things.

- *Waiting for the perfect or just the right set of circumstances.* Unfortunately the perfect set for circumstances rarely occurs. I've heard people say, "When the kids are grown." "When I'm older." "When I have more experience." "When the market is better." "….that's when I'll act." As leaders it is up to us to create the right set of circumstances through our actions.

- *Lack of resources.* Maybe we don't have the money, people, equipment, best players, experience or talent. As leaders it is our responsibility to improve ourselves if that is the area of lack. Maybe we need to train our people. If we have physical needs like money or equipment we can find ways around that or ways to get what we need. Sometimes we just need to think about alternatives. We can use our people's minds and brainstorm possible solutions. I have been amazed at the creativity and solutions that occur when a small group of people begin to brainstorm. One person might come up with a wacky idea but someone else might get an idea from that. Someone else might modify that idea and eventually a solution is born. As leaders through action we can overcome much of the "lack" we think we have.

- *Laziness.* Sometimes it is easier to do nothing. Acting takes work, time and imagination among other things. For the short term it may be more fun and easier to play golf, play video games or watch TV. Taking action may be painful short term but it is the only route to success, long term pleasure and satisfaction.

- *Thinking we don't have the power or authority.* Leaders don't need power and authority. If you learn to lead people will follow. That is what this book is all about. We may feel that we're insignificant or, "What, can I do as just an individual?" but throughout history one person has always made a difference. Think about Christopher Columbus, George Washington, Abraham Lincoln, Susan B. Anthony, Thomas Edison, Franklin Roosevelt, Chuck Yeager, Rosa Parks, John F. Kennedy, Dr. Martin Luther King, Bill Gates, Mother Theresa and Ronald Reagan to name just a few people. The power of one person can literally change history. We shouldn't ever sell ourselves short. We have incredible power if we choose to use it. Believe in yourself and your abilities.

The following true story illustrates how leadership and taking action can make a difference in our world.

The three year old girl lay almost motionless on her hospital bed. The TV with cartoons played in the background. She was tired and sore. She had been poked and prodded almost hourly. The girl had been here for five days with pneumonia and other issues. She needed to start eating and drinking before she could get her IV out if she hoped to go home. But she had no interest in anything especially food. Things weren't looking good and then grandma showed up from out of town. Grandparents sometimes can accomplish feats that parents cannot. In a short period of time grandma had the girl into a chair reading to her. Grandma then coaxed her into a red wagon and they started pulling her down the hall along with her IV. Then the magic really started. Mom was able to get her to drink some juice and then eat a few chips. A troop of Girl Scouts showed up. They had spent their hard earned cookie money on Build a Bears for all of the children in the hospital. A Girl Scout handed the girl a Build a Bear. She smiled and hugged it tightly. Her spirit leaped. A little later a kind lady and her golden retriever showed up. They traveled to hospitals and nursing homes doing "pet therapy." The little girl saw the dog and for the first time in five days stood up on her own in the wagon. After being lifted out of the wagon to the floor, dragging the IV she walked to the dog and gave him a hug. A little later she was running down the hall. Shortly after that she was sent home. Two days later at a follow up doctor's exam everything was normal. Was this sudden turnabout a miracle? I don't know. It does show the power an individual can have and the difference one person can make. When combined with other people incredible things can happen.

The grandmother took some actions that the doctors and nurses choose not to take. She was a leader. Sometimes we worry more about what others think and say than doing what we know is right for us. This takes courage. We may need to overcome fear. We shouldn't ever sell ourselves short. We have incredible power if we choose to use it. We must take action.

THOUGHTS *to ponder and* ACTIONS *to take*

- Do I act or do I procrastinate?

- Is there an action(s) I know that I need to take but have been putting off?

- What is holding me back?

- What is the best thing that could happen if I took this action?

- What is the worst thing that could happen if I took this action?

- What is the most probable outcome if I took this action?

- Today do something toward one of your goals.

- Today take an action you have been putting off.

CHAPTER 5

TRUST

YOU CAN'T LEAD WITHOUT IT.

One question I always ask students in my seminars is, "If your boyfriend (or girlfriend) told you that they had to study for an exam rather than attend a concert with you but you found out on Monday that they were really out with someone else what would you do?" I get answers from, "I would dump them," to "I might give them a second chance." I then ask, "What if next weekend they tell you that they can't go out with you because they have a term paper to finish. What would you do?" I usually get uncomfortable laughter. The typical answer is, "I wouldn't trust them." Once trust is lost it is difficult to regain whether it is boyfriend/girlfriend, Parent/child, husband/wife or leader/followers.

As leaders we need to be able to earn and keep the trust of our people. If people can't believe us will they believe in our vision? Will we get their best if they aren't convinced we can deliver the rewards or results we state or that we will do what we say we will do? It is critical to have the trust of those you lead. Unless they trust you they simply won't follow. If you have a title or position you may get minimal compliance but that's about all. Maybe your people really need the job so they follow you. If another job comes along that looks just a little better they will probably take it. Being able to trust a leader is critical for the success of any high performing and successful team or organization. What is trust and how can we earn it and keep it?

Trust is made up of two major parts--respect and integrity. Treating a leader respectfully is treating them courteously and with simple human dignity because of their position or office or because we should treat all people with politeness and dignity. Having respect *for* a leader is quite different. It means that we may look up to them, maybe even imitate them. If they are our leader we look to them for leadership. Think of the people that you respect what qualities do they have? We may respect them for what they have done for the organization. Maybe they have been successful within the organization as a player or have been very successful managing a segment of the company. They may have a particular talent. We may respect them for their character or what they have done for others. We may respect them for what they have done for us.

One of the most important qualities of a leader and one that earns our respect is integrity. Integrity is being honest. It is also being true to ourselves and our values. It has been said that if we are true to ourselves we can't be false to anyone else. We respect leaders that are true to their own values even if we don't always agree with them. There is a certain comfort following those that are true to their values. We know what to expect.

Pope John Paul II was one of the most popular popes ever in the history of the Catholic Church. People didn't always like or agree with his positions on issues but they knew where he stood and why. They respected his integrity and their disagreement didn't hurt his popularity.

As a leader being true to your values is critical. Remember that you will be judged based on what you do rather than what you say. The first year our high school soccer team went to the state final four, our captain was not always well liked because he made the players work so hard in practice. But they followed him not only because of his vision but because they respected him. He was a good player and had been on the team for four years. He was always out in front leading the drill. He had a good example to follow. Bruce, the head coach not only stays in great physical condition but when the team runs wind sprints, which they hate, Bruce runs right with them. Bruce has never asked his players or us as coaches to do anything he hasn't done or wouldn't do. We respect leaders like this.

Even in industry, I have heard the same comments about great leaders, "He/she wouldn't ask you to do anything they haven't already done or wouldn't do."

We also respect people for their past accomplishments as a leader or as a team player. This may be the successful sales person who becomes the sales manager or the successful player who becomes captain. We know they have been where we are and were successful. We may also respect people for fighting through adversity to achieve their goals or dreams. The greatest influence we have with others is when we don't give up when faced with adversity. But one of the biggest reasons we respect a leader is because they take responsibility for their actions and that of the team or organization rather than blaming people or circumstances. I recently saw a letter the CEO of a large company sent to his employees after a very poor year. The company had four major goals and didn't achieve any of them. In the letter the CEO blamed the employees for the lack of success and threatened them with losing their jobs if things didn't change. What was interesting was he blamed everyone but himself, The Leader. Things didn't change much the next year. As a result some employees were fired, but the best employees left to work for better leaders and organizations. Most likely things will continue to get worse until either the leader changes or gets changed.

The greatest leaders earn respect by taking responsibility for failure but sharing the credit for the team's success. This is particularly true in situations where a player or subordinate does exactly what the leader wants done but things don't work out as planned. In these cases the leader stands behind the player or subordinate making it clear that it was the leader's fault and not the subordinate's. People will accept honest mistakes from a leader with integrity.

Integrity is much more than honesty. It is being true to our word. It is doing what we say we will do. One lady in our church always had great ideas and would set up projects and events. She could even get support to accomplish them. But she would be out of town or wouldn't show up for the events when her leadership and support was most needed. The people involved always managed to get the job done but stopped volunteering if they knew that this woman was involved. She became ineffective as a leader and had to be replaced. If you say that you are going to do something, do it! If you say that you are going to be somewhere at a particular time, be there! There may be things that happen occasionally, but if you consistently fail to walk your talk you will lose respect and be ineffective as a leader.

The worst thing a leader can do is to intentionally lie to their people. This destroys the trust they have built up and causes their followers to question the truth of everything they say. People can deal with the truth even if they don't like it. At least they know how things are. They will still maintain trust and respect for the leader. The situation is the same when a teen lies to a parent or seriously breaks the agreed curfew without a phone call or a man or woman cheats on their spouse. Trust is broken. Once trust is broken, whether between boyfriend and girlfriend, parent and child, husband and wife or leader and followers, it is extremely difficult to get back. It takes a long time to regain trust.

Another way to maintain the trust and respect of others is to not talk openly about things that were told to us in confidence. If we must criticize or correct a subordinate or team member we must do so in private. What we discuss in private stays private. If people can't trust us they won't confide in us. A leader can never be openly critical of or put down one of their people publicly without losing respect. I've known leaders who even made fun of someone in a group when that individual wasn't with the group. Everyone had a good laugh at the time. But the other people were probably thinking, "I wonder what he tells the group about me when I'm not around." Publicly putting down someone hurts the leader through loss of respect and trust. If a leader is going to talk about their people publicly it should be to praise them. This gains respect for the leader if the praise is sincere and specific.

As leaders we must always operate with integrity. We should even strive to avoid situations that can even give the appearance of being dishonest or show a lack of integrity. Our good name is critical to our effectiveness as a leader. People will follow those they trust even if they don't always like them or disagree with them. Being a person of integrity that can be trusted is a basic requirement of an effective leader. Sometimes it hurts to admit we have made a mistake but that is far better than blaming others or even worse lying to our people. If we choose to always be a leader with integrity people will follow us even through adversity.

If as leaders we earn the respect of others through our actions and if we operate with integrity by being honest and true to ourselves and doing what we say we will do we can earn trust and be effective leaders.

THOUGHTS *to ponder and* ACTIONS *to take*

- Do I try to always operate with integrity?

- Do I show respect to others?

- Do I keep things told to me in confidence confidential?

- Do I avoid talking negatively about others behind their back?

- Do I take responsibility for our team's failures and share the credit for success?

- We can't change the past only the future. If you can't answer "yes" to all of the above questions make a decision to change starting today and look at how you are doing on a weekly basis.

CHAPTER 6

TEAMBUILDING

YOU CAN'T DO IT ALONE.

Leaders can't do everything by themselves. They don't have all the talent and they certainly don't have the time. One of the biggest challenges of any leader to is to mold their people into an effective team.

A few years ago I played on West Virginia's "Veterans Cup Team." The Veterans Cup is a national soccer tournament for teams over forty years old. It's a big deal. Each state sends one or two teams depending on their size. That year the tournament was in Beckley, West Virginia but there was no West Virginia team in the tournament. Our soccer club was asked to put an over forty men's team together for the tournament. For three months we practiced together, we played together. We even scrimmaged college teams to get ready for the tournament. When we got to the tournament we lost all three games without even scoring. But we played our last and best game against the team that won the tournament and became the national champion. By that time, we were starting to come together as a real team. A few weeks later our Veterans Cup Team played a team of all stars from our own club. These were guys in their twenties and thirties. All of them had played high school soccer many had played college soccer. They were faster, quicker and most were more skilled than we were. Many of the Veterans had never even played high school much less college soccer. The final score was 5-0 in favor of *the Veterans Cup Team*. The game was so one sided our captain told us late in the game, "Don't shoot anymore just pass the ball around because they're getting mad." As I was changing my shoes I was thinking, "How did that happen?" We were more experienced but more importantly we were a TEAM.

In fairness to the young guys that was the first time they had been on a field together. Teamwork made all the difference. A talented team will always beat a team of all stars. We saw that in the 2004 Summer Olympics in men's basketball. The USA had great players but they couldn't get it together as a Team. As a result for the first time the US failed to win a men's basketball medal.

Industry uses teams on a regular basis. Unfortunately, unless leaders understand how to build strong teams many of these will fail. It's imperative that as leaders we know how to build strong teams.

Books have been written on team building. We won't get into all of the details but we will give you some ideas that will help you as a leader to build successful teams.

Here are the keys to having successful teams;

- <u>A common goal or vision that everyone buys in to</u>. This is the single most important element of a successful team. A friend of mine played on a team that won the state high school football championship the year he was a senior. He said, "The seniors decided that we were going to win the state title and convinced the rest of the team." I asked, "Did you like everyone on the team?" He said, "Heck no. Some of the guys were jerks. But when we got on the field it didn't matter because we were all going for the same goal." One season we had several players on our high school soccer team that for whatever reason just didn't like each other. Sometimes I felt like a ringmaster or referee at practice. But once they all agreed on the goal that we were going to the state final four, our practice sessions changed for the better. On the field we were a unit. One opposing coach even commented in the press that we didn't have any great players but we were a great *Team*. We made it to the final four because a common goal unifies. Every successful team I have been part of, corporate or athletic, always knew what the vision or goal was and committed to it.

    As a young coach, I remember the worst team I ever had. Not only did we lose every game but we lost each game worse than the previous game. We had one very talented player, but I couldn't get him to pass the ball. Our opponents quickly figured out that if they marked him, he couldn't score and since he didn't pass our team couldn't score. This player got hurt late in the season and I was surprised that we played better without him. This player never bought into our team vision. His own success was more important to him. I realized that if a player isn't a team player you are better without them no matter how talented or smart they are. This is very true in the corporate world. I've had to terminate employees because they weren't team players and brought disunity to our work teams. It was a hard but valuable lesson for me to learn.

- <u>Individual and team rewards</u>. What's in it for me? These rewards can be external like a raise or bonus or an individual or team trophy. They can be internal like the satisfaction of winning, knowing that your team accomplished its goal or seeing the championship banner hanging in the gym and knowing you helped to put it there. It is important that there are *both* individual and team rewards. If there are just team rewards individuals may not be motivated to maximum performance. If there are only individual rewards then individuals may not play as team. My son played on a soccer team once where some of the parents we found out were paying their sons $5 for each goal they scored. This destroyed the team as the players were more concerned with their $5 goals than the team winning. They didn't win very often. As a leader, remember praise is also a very effective individual reward. Sometimes one of the reasons people get on a team or volunteer to help an organization is to feel good about themselves. As sad as it is they may not have the opportunity to get praised or feel important anyplace else. No matter what the individual reasons for getting involved are praise is an important reward. Remember team and individual rewards are important.

Several years ago we had a client that was planning a large expansion project. Success was critical so they formed a team with key people from their company and four of their primary vendors. They made sure that everyone understood the goals and what success would look like, but they also did something else that was unique. If goals were exceeded each year they shared a portion of the savings with their employees in the form of a bonus and with each of the vendor companies that had to be given to their employees in the form of a bonus. It couldn't just be put into the corporate treasury. We also had periodic celebration lunches for all involved where everyone was given a small token like a clock, a hat or a portable cooler. The results were incredible. In this organization it was rare to complete a project on time and under budget. On this expansion project all of the goals were met and the projects were completed on time and under budget all four years of the project. Even in the fourth year when we thought we had driven all of the excess costs out of the system, individuals from all five organizations, at all levels, continued to generate ideas that improved efficiencies and found ways to further reduce costs.

In recalling our team meetings, unless someone knew the individuals they would not know the company they worked for because everyone was so focused on the goal. This demonstrates not just the power of a common goal, but the power of team and individual rewards. As a result all five companies and their employees were successful. Everyone not only felt good about their success but they also had their awards and bonus checks to show for it. Needless to say the expansion project was an incredible success.

- Effective Communication. For everyone to feel part of the team they need to know what the vision or goal is. They also need to know how they are progressing as a team and as individuals. Where are we going? Where are we at? Where do I fit in? What do I need to do? These are the questions team members want to know on an on going basis. Good communication can also build team spirit. Communication must be open, honest and caring. It should also be positive. That is team members shouldn't belittle or degrade each other. Nothing should be said behind someone's back that we wouldn't say to their face. There can be no fear so that team members feel safe to present ideas, suggestions, and problems. Conflict is healthy if handled properly. If everyone agrees all the time fear may be present or there may not be sufficient diversity on the team. It is the leader that must make sure effective communication happens.

- Diversity. If a football or soccer team has a great defense they can't win unless they score. It takes both offense and defense to win. If a baseball team has great hitters but no fielding or pitching it probably will lose. Diversity is good on a team. It is the very reason why teams are more successful and productive than individuals. Different skill sets, different ideas, and different ways of thinking make teams successful. This is also a challenge for the leader to put of all of these different, ideas, skills and personalities together to form a team. On the expansion project I discussed earlier each company brought different skill sets to the project. The employees also had different skill sets adding to the diversity.

- <u>Leadership</u>. Every successful team has a leader or leaders. In the corporate world this leader may be appointed or elected. On high school sports teams or clubs typically the seniors take this role. Coaches are leaders but the players also need a peer to follow. The leader casts the vision for everyone to follow. The leader or leaders are also responsible for rewards, communication, and diversity. It is the leader that makes sure the team stays focused. This book is all about what it takes to lead. The point here is that no team or organization is consistently successful without an effective leader or leaders.

It is important to get new team members involved quickly so that can feel part of the team. In an athletic team this might be as simple as passing them the ball in practice or scrimmages. In the corporate world this may mean giving them some responsibilities or tasks to complete for the team. They need the opportunity to show what they can do even if they make mistakes. As the leader be patient, and let them learn from their mistakes. If the leader(s) show confidence in new players or team members they tend to live up to the expectations set for them. On the other hand if they look down on them or are shown no confidence, players tend to live up to those expectations also. Business or other types of teams are no different. New members need to be given responsibilities according to their abilities as soon as reasonably possible so they can begin to feel part of the team. It is important that the leader gives them assignments that they can succeed at so that they can build confidence and feel that they are making a contribution to the team. As a leader it is important for you to see your team members not as they are but as they can be. Everyone has abilities. The first time I did Junior Achievement the teacher warned me, "Mr. Kozera these are low level students." She may have been right about their academics but what I found out after working with them for just a few weeks was that they all had incredible talents. One could tear a motorcycle motor down and put it back together. Another already had his pilot's license. One young lady was skilled with horses. Another had great athletic ability. The challenge for the leader is to determine the skills, talents or gifts people have that can help the team and to use them. The great leaders learn where to put their people and how to develop them so that they can maximize their contribution to the team.

- One of the greatest skills of an effective leader is the ability to build high performing teams that will help him or her achieve their vision. Good leaders know that effective teams multiply the skills or their members and will always accomplish more than a group of individuals. I would always rather have an all star *Team* rather than a team of stars.

THOUGHTS *to ponder and* ACTIONS *to take*

- Do I understand the importance of Team? Am I committed to making my team successful? Am I willing to put the team interests above my interests?

- Do I communicate? Does everyone know the vision and where we stand?

- Do I make sure that there are individual and team rewards?

- This week think about teams I have been on. Were they successful? Why or why not? What would I change if I could?

- This week look at some championship professional teams athletic or corporate. What do they have in common? Watch a video or see them in action live or on TV. Watch the coach. What do they do they makes them champions. Hint; Its more than the talent. Remember our Veterans Cup Team. We didn't have the most talent but we won anyway.

CHAPTER 7

COURAGE

LEADERSHIP IS NOT FOR WIMPS.

Several years ago we took our youth group on a ski trip. I had been skiing for about a year and had never skied a black diamond slope. For the non skiers, black diamonds are the most difficult slopes on a mountain. My reason for not doing a black diamond was simple--*fear*. I had a vision of me sliding down the slope on my back with my skis in the air out of control. My daughter is an encourager and said, "Dad, Dropoff (name of the slope, for a reason) isn't that bad tonight. I think you can do it." I figured I probably needed to give it a try. The top was nice and flat and easy. I skied to the edge of the drop off and looked down. Panic set in. It hadn't looked that steep from the bottom. I thought "Kozera are you crazy." My out of control slide vision was back. My son and daughter were waiting at the bottom and waving. I watched little kids ski past me and right down the hill. I considered my options. I could take my skis off and walk up the hill. It would be a long walk and all the little kids would see this grown man carrying his skis *up* the hill. Boy that would be embarrassing. The only other choice was down the slope. I fixed a vision in my mind of me looking back up the slope from the bottom raising my poles in victory. So, heart pounding, I eased over the edge and down the slope. "No going back now I thought." Slowly I skied across the slope and back again working my way down nice and easy. To my relief, I finally made it down. My kids cheered. I turned, looked back up the slope and raised my poles in triumph.

We continue to be avid skiers as a family, and although I'm not an expert we ski about anything. My fear back then seems silly now. All the fun we have had with family and friends, all the great places we have skied, and all the great conversations with my kids just riding up on the lifts would have never happened if I hadn't overcome my fear on Dropoff that night.

Fear is an important and useful emotion. It is designed to keep us safe. In the military they told us that fear before battle is good. It improves our eye sight and heightens our awareness. It keeps us from being foolish and dangerous to our comrades. But it can also keep us from achieving our full potential and reaching our dreams. We fear many things that hold us back. We fear failure so we set low goals or no goals. We fear making a mistake so we don't try something new. We fear what others may think so we follow the crowd. We fear a potential customer saying "No." so we don't make the sales call. We fear being ridiculed or laughed at. No one will laugh at us if we do what everyone else does. We'll end up average and miss being significant or even great. We fear things like snakes and spiders or public speaking (actually our #1 fear even greater than death) and sometimes even success. I've known people that always do something stupid just when they are on the brink of success. As leaders we fear being criticized or being disliked. We may fear making a decision because it may be wrong so we don't make any decision.

Fear can sometimes be described as;

F*alse*

E*vidence*

A*ppearing*

R*eal*

So how do we overcome those fears that are keeping us from being successful and reaching our dreams? If we do the thing we fear, we can defeat fear. Once I had skied "Dropoff" it was easier to come back and do it again. Fear was eventually gone. If we can eliminate False Evidence with truth or knowledge, fear can be overcome. Positive affirmation or encouragement from someone we trust or our team can help us to believe in ourselves and do what we fear. When my daughter told me "You can do it." I had confidence that I could be successful. Sometimes we need to experience the result we fear and realize that it wasn't so bad after all.

I remember when I was in college, the fear, sweating palms and all, of picking up the phone to ask for a date. After I got rejected a few times, I realized that it hadn't hurt too badly and my fears went away. Once we overcome fear, we gain new self-confidence that can lead us to success. As leaders it sometimes takes courage to set a high goal and announce it to our team. It also takes courage to stand by our beliefs and do what we know is right. Like working hard in practice, our players may not like it at the time, but they will have a different opinion when they see a positive result.

Being a good leader isn't always having our decisions liked. Sometimes we just need to make a decision and move on. No one is perfect. If we make a bad decision learn from it. Just don't repeat it. If we make a mistake it's okay to say, "I made a mistake." Or "I was wrong." Usually, when we admit our mistakes we earn the respect of those we lead. They also know that we're not perfect. They just don't want us to think that we are.

There are students that fear getting good grades because others might think they are a nerd. So they settle for a C rather than getting the A they are capable of. Adults are no different they may choose to stay at the same economic level as their friends rather than going for their dreams. They may fear the changes they may be faced with if they succeed so they stay in their comfort zone. Success always requires change. We must have the courage to change and accept change if we are to lead others.

I still fear jumping off a bridge with a bungee cord tied on my leg and don't plan to overcome it by doing it. I don't see that as a barrier to my dreams. But what fears are keeping us from being great leaders? Are we afraid to lead because we might fail or don't like being in a position to be criticized? What if we choose to overcome just one limiting fear at a time? Being a good leader doesn't mean we'll be without fear. It is having the courage to move forward *in spite of* our fears. It is having the courage to make the best decision possible. It is also having the courage to set a challenging goal. It is having the courage to do what we know in our heart is right even if others may disagree or are critical of us. Courage is tough to muster at times because fear can be so strong. But most important of all, leaders must remain true to their core beliefs. If we are true to ourselves we can't be false to anyone else. At that point we become a leader that people can trust. We can become like a rock giving those we lead a sense of stability and confidence. People follow leaders that they can put their confidence in. You can be that type of leader if you choose to overcome your limiting fears.

This doesn't mean you are never afraid. It means that you do what you know is the right thing to do *in spite of* your fear. We call that courage.

THOUGHTS *to ponder and* ACTIONS *to take*

- What do I fear that is limiting my success?

- This week choose to over come one limiting fear by doing it.

- Do I have the courage to stay true to my own values?

- Do I fear success?

- This week look yourself in the eye and give yourself permission to succeed.

- What do my people fear? What example can I set that will help them to overcome their fears?

CHAPTER 8

INFLUENCE

WHAT YOU DO SPEAKS LOUDER THAT WHAT YOU SAY.

On that cool crisp November night in Wheeling, West Virginia on our first trip to the state high school soccer final four we were down 2-0 after three quarters in that semifinal game to the number 2 ranked team in the state. They were loaded with talent and seniors. In the history our school we had only beaten them twice. To make matters worse they had only given up nine goals all season. There was only twenty minutes left before our dream to play for the state title would evaporate. Our captain and best player, BJ, was down with a leg injury. As the trainer worked on him Bruce, the head coach, came over to see how bad BJ was hurt. As Bruce looked down at BJ with a worried look, BJ pointed his finger at coach, I'll never forget the fire in BJ's eyes, and shouted, "Don't you *dare* take me out coach." Bruce left BJ in. Everyone was tired and many were hurting but whether he realized it or not BJ had sent a clear message to his teammates that even though we were behind and even though he was hurt, he wasn't about to quit. He led his teammates back onto the field. Shortly after that we scored. With less than two minutes to play, BJ hit a shot into the upper right corner of the goal to tie the game and send it into overtime. I don't recall BJ saying much to his players. No great speech. What made the difference was what he *did*. His example said everything and his team followed him to victory against all odds.

Looking back at that season leading by example was common for BJ. He was the hardest working person on the squad. When we ran a drill he led the drill and worked as hard or harder then his players.

Remember how I defined a leader. Anyone that influences people and develops people is a leader. So if you intend to be a leader you must be able to influence people. That is the essence of leadership. You must be able to influence how people think, what people do, and inspire them to follow you. That is exactly what BJ did on that November night in Wheeling. He did it not by what we said but by what he did.

This chapter will discuss how to influence people. Notice I said influence not manipulate. I think of manipulation as getting people to do things they wouldn't normally do or don't really want to do. As a leader always remember that people do things for their own reasons not yours. In general people are worried about themselves and their needs not you and your needs. What leaders do is encourage people to follow them willingly. Great leaders don't need to manipulate people. They show people how to get what they want. Our players all wanted to play for the state championship. It was their dream. They believed that if they followed BJ back onto the field that night they could achieve their dream. They were right.

The following are some of the keys to influencing people;

EXAMPLE

In leadership, example isn't the main thing it's everything. As leaders it is not what we say, it's what we do. We can tell our players to work hard in practice and how important it is to our success as a team, but if we loaf in practice everyone notices and acts accordingly. On the job our followers will rarely work any harder than we do. If we tell the people who work with us that it is critical to get assignments done on time but we can't be on time for a meeting, should we be surprised when assignments get turned in late?

Recently after the passing of Pope John Paul II we heard of how he led by example right to his death. The greatest leaders Jesus, Gandhi, Mother Theresa, Martin Luther King Jr. George Washington, Ronald Reagan General Patten, Pope John Paul II and others all led by example. No matter what your religious belief, if any, Jesus is recognized as a great leader. He took twelve regular guys who had plenty of human flaws, one betrayed him, one denied him, and they started a church that numbers in the millions today. In simple terms leaders influence others and develop people. If you are going to be a leader you must do the same. That is what BJ did. The next season our new leaders followed many of the examples BJ had set and we returned to the state tournament. In the Bible there are a number of classic leadership lessons. One of the best is at the last supper Jesus had on earth where Jesus washed the feet of his disciples. When he was finished he clearly stated, "I have set an example for you…" You can read the entire story in John chapter 13. Great leaders never ask anyone to do anything they haven't done or wouldn't do. They are easy to follow because their lives give their followers a clear picture of what to do.

Remember as leaders our people are always watching us whether we like it or not. It's part of being a leader. What do the people that watch us see? Do we walk our talk? Are our actions consistent with our words? Do we just tell them what to do or do we show them? Remember if we want our people to work hard we must work hard. If we want our people to be on time we must be on time. If we want our people to treat us with courtesy we must first treat them with courtesy. If we want our people to be honest with us we must be honest with them. We can never expect more out of our people than *we* are willing to give. Example isn't the main thing it's everything. That's the good news and the bad news of leadership because it all depends on what kind of example we *choose* to set. We get what back what we give good or bad. We have probably all seen teams or organizations where the leader blamed everyone or everything but themselves. You know the officials, the other team, the weather, the market, bad luck, etc, etc, etc. Of course so did the rest of the team or organization. These teams are rarely successful.

What we *do* always speaks louder than what we *say*. We can choose to follow the examples set by the great leaders and make sure that the example we set is positive and consistent with what we say and will move our team or organization closer to its goal.

As leaders we must always lead by example. Make sure that it is good example.

THOUGHTS *to ponder and* ACTIONS *to take*

- Do I just tell people what to do or do I show them?

- Are my words and my actions consistent with each other?

- Pay special attention this week to what you say and what you do. Are you consistent? What do you need to change?

APPRECIATION

Recently a friend of ours who had been working two jobs decided that her financial condition was such that she could afford to leave one of her jobs. The job she chose to keep was the one with lower pay and less benefits. I asked her why she kept the job she did? She said, "Because I feel appreciated there by my employer and my co-workers. When I leave in the evening, I'm exhausted but I feel like a made a difference to someone that day."

The most effective leaders understand this. Whether in business, athletics or volunteerism they understand appreciated people will go the extra mile for them. In business if you are "the boss" people may work for you whether they are appreciated or not because they need the paycheck. In a volunteer situation appreciation may be the only thing that keeps people working for you because they can always choose to leave and not return.

I am the secretary of a trade association. We have no paid positions. All of the work is done by volunteers. The board members and officers all believe in the work the association does but it takes time and money to be involved. Our president always makes a point to thank people publicly for what they do. It may be helping to put on a meeting, being part of the board of directors, or being a financial sponsor for a meeting. The result is the people continue to volunteer and sponsor and feel good about it.

Appreciation is powerful. Many times as we aren't in a position to reward people financially but we can always let people know what they do is appreciated fulfilling a human need to feel important and needed that money sometimes can't fill. Money is important too because it can be equated to appreciation. In a job situation many times it is one way that people judge if praise is sincere. But in many cases the "Great job," or "Thanks," written on the raise slip is as important as the money. Think of the many people who volunteer in hospitals, churches, scouting, as coaches for young people and in many other civic and service organizations for no money at all. I know people who can't wait to leave work so that they can go to their volunteer work. Is that because they know they are doing something important? Do they know they are making a difference? Every once in a while does someone smile and say "Thanks," like they really mean it. It may be any of these or other reasons. This summer many youth groups and their adult leaders will hit the road to repair homes for those who can't afford to. They will spend their own money or money they took time to raise. They will use their own vacation, time they could have spent having fun at the pool or the beach or playing golf. They will return home exhausted but happy knowing they made a difference in the life of another person.

So what's the point? Whether at work, on the athletic field, at school or at home to be successful we must work with people. Some companies even state, "Our people are our most important asset." Actions always speak louder than words. Do the actions of the leaders and how employees treat each other match the words? I continue to hear that shortages of materials and equipment aren't as important as the shortage of trained people and willing workers. Money and benefits are important but what if we could find a way to tap in to that same spirit that causes people to volunteer, something as simple as sincere appreciation if used effectively can be powerful in building a team, building loyalty and motivating people. Remember as leaders we set the example. If we are appreciative then there is a chance that those that follow us will also be appreciative. Who knows some appreciation might even come our way.

One of the greatest human needs is to feel needed, to feel important. People will go to great lengths to fill this need and will actually die without it. I have watched healthy people die after being retired for six months from a career where they were very important. They had people coming to them daily for decisions and opinions suddenly no one cares about their opinion. They feel unimportant. This is common for the elderly in nursing homes. When they feel they are a burden or have no reason to live they die. There is usually is a physical reason but the main reason is a lack of will to live. They may feel that no one needs them any more. One of the main reasons people leave their jobs or quit volunteering is because they feel unappreciated. The important thing to remember is that people need to feel important, needed or significant. This is true at home, at work or in sports or volunteer organizations. We can meet this need with sincere appreciation. Sometimes we can neglect those closest to us. In the business world people will work for money or recognition. Recognition is the better motivator.

Whenever I ask people about the qualities of the best leaders they have worked for one thing I always hear is, "They appreciate their people." We as leaders can show appreciation in many ways: a card, a small gift, a raise, or a bonus. But a simple smile and a sincere "Thank you," is always effective and welcome. It doesn't cost anything but some time and thoughtfulness. Being appreciative is a great habit to develop as a leader. We all have much to be thankful for; families, friends, our talents and just living in the United States where we have freedom is a great place to start. When we get up in the morning if we start the day being thankful for what we have it will help us to get in the habit of being appreciative. As leaders that time will pay big dividends.

THOUGHTS *to ponder and* ACTIONS *to take*

- Do I see the good that people do and do I appreciate them?

- Do I tell people "Thank you."?

- Do people know that I appreciate what they do for me or the organization?

- Tomorrow when you get up before you get involved for the day, find three things that you are thankful for. Try to make this a daily habit.

- This week make a point to show your appreciation to two people.

- Sometimes we neglect those closest to us. This week tell your spouse, significant other, parent or a close friend, "Thanks" for something they have done for you.

PRAISE

When we work with our high school soccer players one of the things that we work on all season is teaching our players to shoot with both feet. This allows our players to shoot quickly and take advantage of opportunities. In a big playoff game a few years ago we found ourselves behind by two goals. If we lost we would be eliminated. The ball came to Joe, one of our juniors, who had an open goal and the ball on his left foot. But Joe decided not to shoot with his left foot instead he shifted the ball from his left foot to his strong right foot. In that split second two defenders got between Joe and the goal. He shot anyway and the ball bounced harmlessly away. An opportunity lost. I was furious. After all the work we had done in practice, Joe didn't do what we had worked on all season. I considered really going off on him when we took him out. Then I figured he probably realized that he had messed up. My going off wouldn't help. So when I talked to Joe I just told him, "The next time the ball comes to your left foot and you have a shot take it. I don't care where the ball goes." In the second half still down a goal Joe got an opportunity and shot the ball low and just inside the left post to tie the game *with his left foot.* Of course Joe got congratulated by his teammates. He knew he was a hero. When Joe came out at the end of the third quarter I slipped over to him and whispered, "Nice left foot." Joe smiled. We went on to win that game and advance. I never had to say anything to Joe about shooting with his left foot his entire senior season. The message here for leaders is that praise is usually far more effective than criticism.

Praise is a powerful tool for any leader. Your position as leader puts you in a unique position to use praise and really uplift your teammates or subordinates. Many times as leaders we aren't in a position to reward people financially but we can always praise them, which fulfills a human need to feel important and needed, one that money sometimes can't fill. Praise if used effectively can be one of the most powerful tools that any leader can have in building a team, building loyalty, and motivating his people.

Our leading goal scorer one season who was also the leading scorer in the entire state was interviewed by the press who asked him about his ability to score goals. His comment was insightful and effective. He said, "It's not me. It's my teammates that feed me that ball that make me so successful." What happened? Praised publicly in the newspaper his teammates gave him even more passes to set him up and he scored more goals. Public praise is even more effective. Remember people will repeat the act they get praised for because praise feels good and so does knowing you did something right.

For praise to be effective it must be done properly otherwise it will appear as flattery, which is de-motivating and more importantly causes the leader to look insincere and damages his integrity.

FOR PRAISE TO BE EFFECTIVE IT MUST BE

Sincere-We need to mean what we say. We need to be honest.

Specific-The person being praised knows exactly what they are being praised for.

Praise the act not the person-We always praise what a person does that they can control. They can always choose between *any* number of acts. We want them to know that we are not only aware of but appreciated this particular action.

Whenever possible explain the positive results that occurred because of their actions.

PRAISE PUBLICLY WHENEVER POSSIBLE.

What might this look like? Let's say you are captain of the basketball team and one of your players is standing at their locker on Monday morning with one of their friends. As you pass by you smile and say, "Thanks for that great pass on Friday. We wouldn't have made the game winning basket without it." The praise is sincere. They can see it in your face and tone of voice. It's specific, "that great pass." The act "pass" was praised not the person. The result was stated, "The game winning basket." Finally it was public. That person may look more important in the eyes of their friend because "the captain" took the time to praise them. The result is a more loyal team member who will probably be willing to pass to others.

One of the greatest human needs is to feel needed and to feel important. People will go to great lengths to fill this need. The main reason people leave their jobs isn't money, most of the time it's because they feel unappreciated. In my work with high school students, I always ask my classes, "How many of you have been praised for something you did in the last two weeks?" I usually get a few hands. Then I ask, "How many of you have been criticized for something you did in the last two weeks?" Every hand in the room is up. The message for leaders is that people don't get enough sincere praise. If you are observant that is a need that you can fill and in the process become a stronger more effective leader. Many managers don't believe in praise because, "The people might ask for a raise." They mistakenly believe that fear and criticism will keep people in line and working. If these work at all their effect is short term. Leaders understand that how to positively motivate people so that they will *want* to give their best to the organization.

So what if someone messes up or they do something we don't like? Dale Carnegie in his book *How to Win Friends and Influence People,* which has been in print for over seventy years, says to never criticize. People don't like criticism and they get very defensive. If we do need to criticize it should always be done privately and we criticize the act not the person. The worst thing a leader can do is to embarrass someone in front of the group. It makes both the leader and the person being embarrassed look bad. It normally doesn't change long term behavior. It may demoralize the person criticized making them ineffective for the team. It creates fear among the group that they may be next to get embarrassed creating lack of initiative and even inaction. But as leaders we have an obligation to help our people.

If they are making mistakes they must know about them and how to fix them. I call this coaching. The important thing to remember is that people need to feel important, needed or significant. As leaders we can meet this need with praise. In the business world people will work for money or recognition. Recognition is always the better motivator.

As a coach one of the hardest things I had to learn to do was to praise and encourage a player after a tough loss when they had played the best they could. I used to say, "Good game." That came across as a negative because they would say, "We lost coach." To be effective I had to be specific in my praise. So I might say to the goal keeper, "That was a tough loss but you made some great saves that kept us in the game." Another thing we can do is say how we felt about something and give our opinion which can't be disputed. For instance, "Guys, that was a tough loss but I like the way you continued to play hard and never quit." This can also be an effective way to avoid being judgmental. I can always honestly tell my wife that I like her outfit or the way she did her hair. She may not agree with me if she isn't satisfied with her hair but what I like or dislike is my choice and can't be disputed. This may be a good way to respond if someone asks, "Does this outfit make me look fat?" It is far safer to respond that we either like or dislike how the outfit makes them look.

In today's world as leaders electronic communication is common. The same thoughts apply. Never send a negative e-mail criticizing someone even if you think it is only going to one person. I have been on the distribution list for negative e-mail that has been spread around an entire company and was only intended for one person. Sometimes we say things in the heat of a moment that we wouldn't say once we calmed down. However, once we hit "send" it's too late to recall the message. If I receive a negative e-mail rather than respond online and create a negative e-mail war, which will happen. If it is worth responding to, I will call the sender and discuss the matter one on one. If we want to praise someone's actions or thank them for their efforts e-mail is a great way to do it especially if we copy higher management or in sports the head coach. Remember praise publicly. For some reason, I notice that negative e-mail gets forwarded faster than positive email. That's okay. Just keep your e-mails positive.

The ability to praise is one of the most effective skills that any leader can have. But like any other skill it needs to be practiced to be effective. If we look hard enough we can find something good that everyone has done. We can look for the good or the bad. Start to practice looking for the good or those things that someone has done right. If you are uncomfortable with praise maybe starting with a family member or a friend would be helpful. Many times it is those closest to us that we praise the least. You might start with something simple like, "I really liked your dinner tonight." Or to your wife or girlfriend (husband or boyfriend), "I really like your new outfit." Just be sincere, be specific and praise the act or action. Just like in my example with Joe the leader can raise moral and improve the performance of their people. The effects can be long lasting.

THOUGHTS *to ponder and* ACTIONS *to take*

- Do I praise my people or just criticize?

- Can I praise more frequently?

- Do I look for what people do right or just look for mistakes?

- How do I respond to negative e-mails if I am upset?

- *Today* effectively praise a loved one or a close friend for something they have done.

- *Tomorrow* look for something positive one of my subordinates or team members has done and effectively praise them for it.

TREAT PEOPLE RIGHT

A good friend of mine had spent a month in Europe with his family where they visited most of the countries. I was curious how they dealt with the language barrier. My friend told me, "We only spoke English but before we entered any country we learned two words in their language, *please* and *thank you*. We never had any trouble." I was amazed. *Please* and *Thank You* got my friend and his family through Europe. Those words are just as powerful for us as leaders. If you need to have something done always ask someone to *please* help you or do what you need rather than telling someone to do it or demanding to have it done. This is important especially if you actually have the authority to demand compliance. This also separates managers from leaders. Leaders know that they don't need to command and most people don't like to be told what to do. Quality is usually better if people do things willingly. If you are in a volunteer situation you will learn quickly that if you act like a jerk and demand compliance some people will tell you, "Stick it."

The others will just leave. Then nothing gets done or you get to do it all yourself.

Always treat people with the dignity and respect they deserve as human beings. Think of how you would prefer to be treated and act accordingly.

THINK WIN/WIN

One thing I learned by being associated with the National Speakers Association is when we are on the platform, "It's not about us. It's all about the audience." This one simple premise turned my public speaking around. It's the same for any leader. Zig Zigler, speaker, author, trainer and sales expert says, "We can have anything we want if we first help enough other people get what they want."

When I was a kid our neighbor, Mr. H_, was a real piece of work. He was always trying to get something for nothing. One Saturday he had a load of logs dumped for his fireplace. They were huge. Most were two or three feet in diameter and needed to be split so they could fit in his fireplace. In those days the only way to split wood was with a wedge and a sledge hammer. It was hard work. As kids we hung out with Mr. H_ because he let us do things our parents wouldn't let us do at home like paint and use power tools. Occasionally he would even pay us for the work we did.

My brother, John, and I were splitting the wood hoping to get paid. Our friend Ritchie came walking down the road. Ritchie was two years older than me and lifted weights. Mr. H_ shouted, "Hey Ritchie look at how fast John can split this wood." Ritchie looked at John swinging the sledge hammer and said, "I can do better than that." He grabbed a sledge hammer and a wedge and started splitting wood. Shortly after that, Gary, another one of our friends came walking down the road. He started watching us work and laughed. Gary and Ritchie were friends and also natural competitors. Mr. H_ yelled at Gary, "Hey Gary look how strong Ritchie is and how fast he can split a log." Gary growled, "Give me a hammer." He was soon working his fanny off trying to out split Ritchie. Soon all the wood was split and it didn't cost Mr. H_ a dime. He was certainly a winner but what about us? We won too. We actually enjoyed trying to outwork each other especially Ritchie who outworked Gary to become champion log splitter. We could have walked anytime but chose not to. Because Mr. H_ understood kids, he got his logs split for free and we actually had a good time. As leaders we always need to look for ways everyone can win. There are always possibilities if we look for them just like Mr. H_ did.

My daughter has a friend who is a grade school principal. The principal was having trouble with one of her teachers who was getting burned out. This was not good for the teacher, the kids or the principal. The woman was talented but her performance had deteriorated to the point that it looked like she would have to be terminated or transferred. However, this principal was a leader and understood how to look for the win/win. The problem teacher enjoyed reading to children and was good at it. The principal found a way to move this problem teacher into the library where she could read to children. In the end the kids won, the teacher won, and the principal won. The principal chose to not take the easy way out and used her creativity to create a win/win result.

Remember that a win/lose eventually becomes a lose/lose. If you ever think you got something over on someone keep your eyes open because what goes around comes around. There is always a renegotiation and eventually you will find yourself on the losing end. On the athletic field one team wins and one team loses. But as leaders one of the best ways to influence people to do what we want on an ongoing basis is to make sure that they win by getting what they want when they follow us.

THOUGHTS *to ponder and* ACTIONS *to take*

- Do I look for win/wins?

- Do I understand that people do things for their own reasons, not mine?

- Do I treat people with respect and dignity, like I prefer to be treated?

- This week focus on the other persons needs first and look for ways that we can both be successful and win.

CHAPTER 9

RESPONSIBLITY
TAKING THIS WILL ACTUALLY GIVE YOU CONTROL.

As a young new manager, my facility had a terrible safety record. We were bad. I don't think we went a month without a reportable incident. When my regional manager called, I always had an excuse why things were happening and why it wasn't my fault. When he called after a particularly serious accident, I started in to my excuses when he cut me short and began to verbally rip me apart. He told me, in no uncertain terms, that I was responsible for the safety of my people and it was time to quit making excuses and do something about safety. I remember being upset and thinking about how unfair my regional manager had been. I thought what could I do? However, as I thought about it and swallowed the bitter pill that maybe he was right, things changed. Once I, as the leader, *took responsibility* for our local safety program the leaders under me began to take responsibility in their areas. Things began to change. We quit being powerless victims. We realized that there was a lot that we could do. In a remarkably short time our location's safety record went from one of the worst to one of the best. Our men drove one million and then two million miles without an accident. We previously thought that this was impossible for us. It became normal. The key was the leader taking responsibility for his actions and the rest of the leadership team followed. This set the example for each individual.

Taking responsibility is difficult, but it is critical for our success and growth. Taking responsibility is essential for an effective leader. The alternative is to blame someone or something. Unfortunately all that we have control over is ourselves.

Taking responsibility for our actions means taking control of our lives. As long as we blame others or circumstances, we are powerless until the others change or circumstances change. This is critical for a leader to know. People look to leaders for direction. As leaders we are expected to make things happen no matter what the circumstances. It has been said that success is only 10% what happens to us and 90% how we deal with it. We need to be able to influence others and develop people. Great leaders don't sit around waiting for the right circumstances to occur. If need be they create the circumstances they need to succeed.

People follow leaders they feel are confident and in control. They know that if there are difficulties (and there always will be) they want a leader they know will get them through. To be in control as leaders, we must take responsibility for ourselves *and* our people. Even though I wasn't having accidents my people were. I needed to take responsibility for creating circumstances where they could be safe. This sometimes meant making tough decisions, especially dealing with people. As leaders sometimes we need to help our people take responsibility for their actions. If my people aren't performing, I am responsible for helping them to improve their performance. Our people are also responsible for their actions. Unfortunately sometimes people choose to do things that hurt the team. If we can't change them we may need to remove them from the team for the good of the team or put them in a position when they have minimal impact on the team. We saw this recently in the NFL with Terrell Owens, a great talent who wouldn't talk to his quarterback. His coach decided the team was better off without his talent.

A few years ago our high school soccer team suffered a tough loss in a big game. One of the underclassmen remarked after the game, "The refs stole this one from us." One of our senior leaders quickly jumped in and said, "No. We lost because we didn't play as well as we could." I was so proud of him. This leader accepted responsibility for the result (the loss). He realized that in order to be successful we had to find a way to win no matter who the referees were. As a result of this leader and our other seniors taking responsibility for our results instead of blaming the referees, some individual (scapegoat) or circumstances, like luck, they were able to keep control of our team's destiny. They chose to be powerful rather than powerless. As a result we had a great season. More important they showed the underclassmen by their example how important it was to take responsibility. The underclassmen learned that they couldn't blame others, like the referees, for their poor performance. When these underclassmen became seniors they knew the importance of taking responsibility.

As leaders it is important that we take responsibility for ourselves and our team or business unit. By taking responsibility we take control of our destiny. Great leaders find a way to be successful in spite of the circumstances. A good friend of mine is remarkably successful. She has a great family. She owns her own company that is doing very well. She is friendly and happy. She is the kind of person people like to be around. When she was a child her father left her. Her family was dirt poor. She was abused. Yet in spite of her circumstances she became successful. Why? She said, "I knew that once I turned eighteen I could do and be whatever I chose to do and be." This young woman could justifiably blame her parents or circumstances and live as a victim. Instead she chose to rise above her circumstances and take responsibility for her own life. The result was incredible success. That is exactly what we need to do as leaders. We can't always control our circumstances we can always control how we choose to react to them.

When people talk of those leaders that had the greatest impact on their lives and that they have the greatest respect for one of the qualities they always mention is that they back up their people. If you did what the leader asked and if things went wrong the leader took full responsibility and made sure upper management knew it was his decision. I have seen managers lose the respect of their people when one of their people was chewed out in a meeting for doing something the manager had them do and the manager stayed silent and failed to take any responsibility. As leaders we can choose to delegate our authority but the responsibility is always ours.

To be a successful leader we must take responsibility for our actions and the actions of those we lead. Remember when we take responsibility we also take control of our destiny.

THOUGHTS *to ponder and* ACTIONS *to take*

- Do I take responsibility or do I blame other people or circumstances for my failures?

- Do I look for the things that I can do to change my circumstances?

- This week think about a situation where you felt like you were the victim of circumstances or others actions. Look for the things that you have control of like your attitude and your actions. Think about what you can do that might create a different more favorable outcome?

CHAPTER 10

DEVELOPING PEOPLE AND FUTURE LEADERS

INVESTING TIME IN PEOPLE PAYS BIG DIVIDENDS.
PASS ON WHAT YOU KNOW.

On the night in Wheeling in 1999 we went into overtime tied at 2 goals each. Fortunately for us the rules required that the entire overtime period be played even if one team scored. Our opponent had scored first. Time was running out on us. With thirty seconds left our opponent kicked the ball deep to try to run out the clock. Tony our goalie came way out of net and chest trapped the ball. He got it to Nathan at midfield who quickly passed it to Stewart who crossed it to BJ our senior captain with just ten seconds left. BJ wanted to win this game badly. But instead of taking the shot BJ dropped it to little Kenny, *a freshman*. Kenny was only about five feet tall. The only reason he was on the field that night was because the upper classman starter playing that position was injured during the game. BJ chose to put his dream in Kenny's hands (or foot in this case). Kenny shot and put the ball in the net with just one second left! We won the game in a shootout and played for the State Championship the next day. BJ had faith that Kenny could score and he did. That is how leaders develop people. It was no accident that Kenny had developed through the season so when his moment came he was ready. Bruce, our head coach, is great at developing his players. BJ as a leader had helped that development. It paid off in a big way.

Remember that leaders influence and develop people. To develop people we need to teach, train and coach. Teaching explains new concepts or skills. Training practices those concepts or skills. Coaching lets people know what they are doing right and where they need to improve. To grow and develop people need to use what they learn by taking on some responsibility. In the energy industry we train people to operate expensive high pressure pumping equipment. A new employee can watch someone run the equipment but at some point they need to put their hands on the throttle and run it by themselves. This is not without some risk of failure. One of the greatest challenges of any leader is to know when and how to do this. We don't have the time here to get into detailed training procedures. The best leaders master this skill. As a manager I recall people that wanted to get ahead knew which crews to get on to get the best training. These were also the crews that promoted the most people out. As a leader if you develop people you may lose them as they get promoted. But you will also gain a reputation as a leader that promotes people. The best, brightest and most ambitious will want to be on your team.

When our fall soccer practice starts we always have some of our graduates come back to help with practice before they go off to college. Recently when I got the seniors together after a practice I asked one of the graduates if he had any advice for them. He said, "Get your new players involved from the beginning. Make sure that you pass them the ball in drills or scrimmages even if they make mistakes because they have to learn." This is especially true in business. When new people are ready give them assignments they can succeed at to build their self confidence. Understand that they will make mistakes. This is not the time to chew them out. This is the time to coach. You want people to learn from their mistakes. Always make sure to give people opportunities to grow and develop.

As a leader always make sure that you constantly develop yourself. We never quit learning. Here are some ideas that may help you.

- Read books about leadership and working with people. Leaders are readers. Reading this book is a great start.

- Talk to other leaders. Find opportunities to get around successful leaders. Who we hang out with is who we become.

- Go to conferences and seminars to learn more about leadership.

- Listen to tapes and CDs by successful leaders or others that you can learn from.

Remember as a leader you set the example. If you are always working to get better others on your team may do the same.

THOUGHTS *to ponder and* **ACTIONS** *to take*

- How do I treat my new people? Am I willing to get them involved and try what they learn?

- How willing am I to allow my new people to make mistakes?

- Do I try to hold my people back so I can keep them or do I want to see them grow and develop and maybe even get promoted away from my team?

- Do I work to develop my own leadership skills?

- Today take an honest look at how you develop people. Decide to make a change in an area you need to improve and then DO IT.

CLOSING THOUGHTS

So there you have my thoughts on leadership and what I have seen successful leaders do. Now it's up to you. To be successful at anything it's not about what we know it's about what we do. As a potential leader you must now act. Start with your character. Be a person of integrity. Be a person that can be trusted. Don't be just a talker be a doer. Show your people by setting the example. Have a vision of what you want and a plan to achieve it. Believe that you will succeed. Then work the plan. Build a team to help you and when things get tough or you suffer a set back don't quit. Get up and try again.

Remember when you do succeed that success can be a fleeting thing. Enjoy it. Celebrate it with your team but know that on January 2nd most people don't care what you did last year their concern now is this year. In sports you may have had a great season and won a championship but next year when the season starts your team is 0-0 again. But there are some things that last. The people we influence and develop will go on long after us. Most of the ideas presented in this book weren't new and weren't even mine. They came from leaders I have worked under or associated with like my parents, gym teachers, high school coaches, teachers, college professors, leaders I have worked for and other leaders that I have been associated with or read their work. I respect all of these people and have been fortunate that they came into my life. What lives will you impact positively because of your leadership?

The key to your success as a leader is your people. Always remember to see them not as they are but as they can be. Don't ever be intimidated by the talent of your people, use it, encourage it, develop it, let it shine. Great leaders aren't afraid to let others succeed. They know that when their people or team succeeds so do they. Surround yourself with great people especially those whose skills compliment your own.

Avoid criticism and be lavish with praise. Be a great coach. Share your vision. Let your people see your passion. Be a great communicator not just by speaking and writing but also by listening. This is how we learn and send the message to our people that they are important because we care enough to listen to them. I have heard it said that no one cares what you know unless they first know that you care.

Great leaders listen far more than they speak. Don't be afraid to admit when you are wrong. (You will never always be right.) Finally have and maintain a great attitude. Keep your attitude positive. Negative can destroy an organization or team. Your attitude will be contagious so smile.

I received my copy of the following letter from the mother of one of our former high school soccer players. Bill played in that exciting November state soccer semifinal game in 1999. He was our captain the following season and a great leader who led our team back to the final four. He is currently a medical student and came back to help coach our school's girls high school soccer team before his college started. He wrote this letter to encourage his team before the playoffs. He is still a great leader. What was encouraging to Bruce and me is the leadership values we taught in our "Senior Leadership Minutes." They are apparent in his letter.

Dear beloved CCHS girl's soccer team,

We have reached that time of the year when we separate the women from the girls, and I know that you guys are up to the task. I have been updated throughout the year on your progress and it sounds like we have done quite well, we have won or been very competitive in every game. Now I know that you are aware that what you have accomplished doesn't really mean anything if you don't do well in the playoffs, so I'll spare you that whole ordeal. However, I think that the state tournament should still be our goal, sectional titles are great and all but you will always wonder "what if" if you don't get that regional plaque. Considering, I was part of the most successful boys team in Catholic history (not to brag.....ha), I figured that there are a few things you should take with you into your postseason run.

1.) Don't underestimate any opponent. Teams that you crushed in the regular season can and will put up a fight against you. Talent only goes so far, and effort and determination can put inferior teams into a game with you if you are not ready.

2.) At the same time, do not overestimate anyone. At the beginning of the year I was talking to Kim about why this team has consistently lost to Capitol in the tourney. It's simply because you have placed that team on such a high pedestal that sometimes I honestly don't think you believed in yourself to get the job done. Let me tell you now that this Catholic team should not look at any opponent and not expect to win. Confidence is not cockiness, and you must be a confident team going into every game. Expect to win, and don't accept anything less. If you get down early, do not panic, just play your game, and your skills and hard work will pay off by the time it is over. Obviously people make mistakes, but what separates good teams from championship teams is how we carry ourselves after a mistake. Champions will be able to look their teammates in the eye on the field and the message can be sent without a spoken word. Anytime you step on that field, your teammates and your opponents should be well aware that you are not leaving with anything but a win.

3.) Give it everything you have until the final whistle. In our state semifinal my junior year, we scored in overtime with one second left to force a shootout, it was the third time in the game we had come back. We won the shootout. Whoever wants the games more in the later rounds will win, hands down. As I said earlier, talent only carries you so far.

4.) Finally, have fun! This is what you've worked your butts off for all season. Those early season miles when you all wanted to puke, the hot days, the big wins, the tough losses; all have prepared you for the postseason. It's a whole new season now, the title is yours for the taking. Play as a team, have faith in each other, and have a blast doing it. Play hard but relaxed, playing nervous is not fun. Freshman, don't get nervous out there, you have performed well all season, nothing should change about that now.

Good Luck

Go Irish,

Coach Bill

Remember as a leader you will make a difference in peoples' lives. Make it a positive difference. I believe in you. You can be whatever you choose. Choose to not just be a leader, be a great leader.

WHAT NOW?

So you decided that you want to be a leader. Maybe even a great leader. You understand that the ability to lead is a choice. You have read all that I have had to say about leadership. You might be thinking. What now? How can I best start to use this stuff?

Here are some thoughts that may help.

1. Hang out with great leaders and learn from them. We tend to become like our friends or the people we spend time with.

2. Read books by or about great leaders. Listen to tapes or CDs on leadership. We will be the same as were are now in five years except for the people we spend time with and the books be read.

3. Practice leadership at every opportunity. Accept assignments that give you an opportunity to lead. Join volunteer organizations and become active. All organizations usually need help. If you are active and involved the opportunities to chair a committee or become an officer will present themselves. If you can successfully lead volunteers (They can leave if they don't like you.) you can lead on the job.

4. Find a mentor. This is someone who will guide you, encourage you and be honest with you. You should be able to trust your mentor. You should also be comfortable communicating with them.

Remember a leader is anyone that influences others and develops people. Leadership can come from anywhere in an organization. Leadership is not dependent on title or position. Leadership can be learned.

As a new leader you will make mistakes. That's okay. Learn from them. Admit them. You are not perfect and never will be. Don't be too hard on yourself. That is why practice is so important. Continue to assess your progress and change the things that you need to change.

Finally and maybe most important believe that you can and will become a great leader. We are all constantly evolving and hopefully improving. We need to see ourselves becoming a great leader so that our powerful subconscious mind can help us. We are the product of our thoughts and our choices. The great author and speaker, Earl Nightingale said, "We become what we think about." We can choose to carry positive and uplifting thoughts just as easily as negative thoughts. Keep your thoughts and self talk positive. See yourself becoming a great leader. You can do it.

Printed in the United States
68693LVS00002B/1-150